SAP HANA

Interview Questions
You'll Most Likely Be Asked

Job Interview Questions Series

 Vibrant Publishers

www.vibrantpublishers.com

SAP HANA Interview Questions
You'll Most Likely Be Asked

ISBN-10: 1490318682
ISBN-13: 9781490318684

Library of Congress Control Number: 2013910061

Vibrant Publishers books are available at special quantity discount for sales promotions, or for use in corporate training programs. For more information please write to **bulkorders@vibrantpublishers.com**

Please email feedback / corrections (technical, grammatical or spelling) to **spellerrors@vibrantpublishers.com**

To access the complete catalogue of Vibrant Publishers, visit **www.vibrantpublishers.com**

Contents

This page is intentionally left blank

SAP HANA Interview Questions

Review these typical interview questions and think about how you would answer them. Read the answers listed; you will find best possible answers along with strategies and suggestions.

This page is intentionally left blank

General Overview

1: What led to the invention of SAP HANA technology?
Answer:
The following led to the invention of SAP HANA technology:
   a) Information explosion where data was growing massively from Gigabytes to Terabytes to Petabytes and business required analytics based on this enormous data
   b) Instant data access anytime and anywhere became the customer need to make real time decisions
   c) Business required a flexible way to analyze current and historic information for various reporting solutions

2: Which technologies did SAP HANA evolve from?
Answer:
SAP HANA evolved by combining earlier developed technologies, BW Accelerator and Max DB with its in-memory capabilities.

3: Is SAP HANA a software or hardware?
Answer:
SAP HANA is a combination of hardware and software; it is delivered as an optimized appliance in co-operation with SAP's hardware partners for SAHANA.

4: What are the main components in SAP HANA?
Answer:
The main components of SAP HANA are:
   a) SAP In-Memory Database (IMDB)
   b) In-Memory Computing Studio and
   c) Data Replication components (SLT, BODS, etc.)

5: What is SAP HANA?
Answer:
SAP HANA is an in-memory technology supported by column-based storage and high data compression that allows processing of massive volumes of data and high speed business reporting. It allows its customers to explore and analyze huge volumes of data

from any data source in real time with unprecedented performance. In comparison to traditional RDBMS systems, it is much simpler and faster.

6: What are the capabilities and benefits that HANA offers?
Answer:
   a) Real Time data
   b) Faster queries on large volumes of data
   c) Flexible modeling
   d) Minimized data duplication
   e) No aggregate tables

7: What are the basic technology concepts in SAP HANA?
Answer:
The basic technology concepts in SAP HANA are:
   a) **In-Memory** where data resides on main memory than on disk
   b) **Colum based database,** Data Compression and Pushing application logic to the database layer
   c) **Parallel processing and multi-core CPUs** leveraging the new hardware technology

8: What is the benefit of In-Memory in SAP HANA?
Answer:
The main benefit of using in-memory database is that accessing data from main memory is much faster than accessing data on disk. A very high-speed bus connects the main memory directly to the processors, whereas in hard disks a chain of buses and controllers are involved.

9: Why is SAP HANA fast?
Answer:
SAP HANA is fast for the following reasons:
   a) HANA stores information in electronic memory as compared to regular RDBMS technologies that store information on hard disks

b) Besides, most SAP systems have the database on one system and a calculation engine on another, and they pass information between them. With HANA, all this happens within the same machine

10: What is columnar storage and how does it support faster access of data?

Answer:
Columnar database stores data in a sequence of columns; the entries of a column get stored in contiguous memory locations. This phenomenon is called columnar storage.

Column store is optimized for READ; only the selected columns will be read during query processing, hence it performs well. It offers significant advantages of data compression or encoding data into fewer bits allowing larger volumes of data in main memory and higher performance in selection and aggregation queries.

11: Are column-based tables always better than row-based tables?

Answer:
No. There are business cases where row based tables are advantageous over column, like in frequently updated databases. If the database is frequently updated or inserted, row-based tables perform faster as they are optimized for write operations.

12: What is the difference between row store and column store?

Answer:
The row store is optimized for WRITE operations and is easy to insert/update. All data has to be read during selection, even if only a few columns are involved in the selection process.

Compared to this, the column store is optimized for performance of READ operations and do not support easy insert/update. After selection, selected rows have to be reconstructed from columns.

13: Can you have row store tables in SAP HANA?

Answer:
HANA can have column or row stores; there is no technical limitation. If you have row-store table in HANA, you cannot create any column views on top of those tables. Typically, Metadata or rarely accessed data is stored in a row-store format.

14: How do you decide if the table should be row or column store in your project?
Answer:
If you want to populate the tables with huge amounts of data that should be aggregated and analyzed fast and benefited from compression mechanisms, then column store is a better option. If you want to report on all the columns, then row store is more suitable.
Simple rule of thumb in HANA is 'use a column table unless specified.

15: How does insert or update work faster in HANA environment?
Answer:
SAP HANA do not write directly into column store tables while inserting or updating the data as column store is not optimized for write operations. It first writes the data into a row store buffer which is write-optimized and hence faster. It then takes that data, restructures it and pushes it into a column-oriented store. As a final step, it pushes this restructured columnar data into the main column-oriented table. By following this process, SAP HANA makes use of the row store for write operations to ensure faster performance.

16: What degree of data compression is expected in SAP HANA?
Answer:
The degree of data compression depends on the number of unique values in the data; the fewer the unique values, the better the data compression.

17: What is Delta Merge and how does it support faster read operations?

Answer:
Delta merge moves the data from WRITE optimized Delta memory to READ optimized and compressed Main memory. It transforms the data into an optimized format in terms of memory consumption and read performance. By merging the data into the main storage which is column store, read operations would be faster.

18: What are the different ways of performing delta merge operation?

Answer:
Delta Merge can be done automatically by using Smart Merge technology or manually using MERGE DELTA OF function in SQL statement or using right click option in HANA studio.

19: When you run a query before delta merge, will you lose the data in the delta storage in the result set?

Answer:
No. During any read operation data is always read from both main and delta storages and result set is merged.

20: What is memory latency and how does it hit the performance?

Answer:
While executing any application logic on the data, the application has to get the data from the database, process it, and possibly send it back to the database to store the results. Sending data back and forth between the database and the application usually involves communication overhead and is limited by the speed and throughput of the network, this is memory latency.

21: How does SAP HANA handle the latency problem?

Answer:
In SAP HANA, the calculations and application logic are done at

the database level thereby eliminating the exchange of intermediate results between the database and the application. This minimizes the communication and data transfer between database and application thereby reducing the overall processing time.

22: How does SAP HANA support parallel processing?
Answer:
SAP HANA leverages the multi-core processors, multi-processor servers and scales out into a distributed landscape to support parallel processing.

23: Which are the top use cases in SAP HANA?
Answer:
The top use cases of SAP HANA are:
   a) Real-time Financial Planning
   b) Customer Segmentation
   c) Genome Analysis
   d) Profitability Analysis and
   e) Detective HANA

24: What is the difference between SAP BWA and SAP HANA?
Answer:
SAP BWA is only for SAP BW data; its main aim is to accelerate a portion of the BW data which is crucial for business reporting.
SAP HANA is much more than BWA, it replicates data from SAP ECC, BW or any other non-SAP sources. Besides faster reporting, HANA supports flexible modeling and change management.

This page is intentionally left blank

Architecture

25: What are the primary prerequisites for SAP BW on HANA?

Answer:

The primary prerequisites for SAP BW on HANA are:
    a) Upgrade to SAP Net Weaver 7.02 or above
    b) Migrate database (RDBMS) to HANA DB

26: What is the Operating System requirement for SAP HANA?

Answer:

SUSE Linux Enterprise Server

27: Can HANA Server be configured via Scale up or Scale out configurations?

Answer:

Yes, SAP HANA can be configured via Scale up and Scale out.

28: Name the servers operational in a HANA database.

Answer:

The different servers operational in a HANA database are:
    a) Index Server
    b) Preprocessor Server
    c) Name Server
    d) Statistics Server

29: What is the role of each server in the HANA database?

Answer:

   a) **Index server** plays the prime role; it holds all the data and performs the query operations.
   b) **Preprocessor server** processes the unstructured data and is typically used for Text Data Analysis.
   c) **Name server** holds the landscape information. In a distributed system, name server contains the statuses of the active components and the data located on each server.
   d) **Statistics server** collects the information related to performance and resource consumption.

30: What are the different services present in the HANA

appliance?
Answer:
The different services present in the HANA appliance are SAP Host Agent, Software Update Manager (SUM), SAP CAR, LM Structure.

31: What is the functionality of SUM and LM structures?
Answer:
SUM allows automatic download and installation of SAP HANA versions and upgrades from SAP Marketplace.
LM structure holds details on the current product version installed.

32: Which component coordinates and tracks the database transactions?
Answer:
Transaction Manager coordinates and tracks the database transactions in SAP HANA.

33: How is an application query processed by the Index Server in SAP HANA?
Answer:
The client requests in the application layer are passed down as SQL statements to the Request Processing and Execution Control components. The SQL Processor accepts the incoming SQL requests and executes the same as per the plan generated by the SQL Optimizer.

34: What is the role of MDX engine in the HANA server?
Answer:
Multidimensional query requests from OLAP systems or analytical applications are processed by the MDX engine. Multidimensional data is stored in cubes and can only be queried using the MDX language.

35: Which are the two relational engines in In-Memory

Computing Engine (IMCE)?

Answer:

The two relational engines in IMCE are:
   a) Row store
   b) Column store

Both row store and column store are in-memory databases.

36: What are the key architecture points to be considered to ensure business continuity?

Answer:

The key architectural points that ensure business continuity are:
   a) High Availability per Data Center
   b) Disaster Tolerance between Data Centers

37: How does HANA hardware support High Data Availability?

Answer:

The Scale Out architecture with Standby node, delivered by the hardware partners Fujitsu, HP, IBM, etc. support high data availability in SAP HANA. Different servers are tightly connected to work together as a single system or cluster in this scale out approach and this improves performance and availability.

38: How is HANA hardware structured towards Disaster Tolerance?

Answer:

Server Clustering forming a distributed landscape ensures effective disaster tolerance in HANA environment. The nodes in a cluster would be stationed at different locations, thereby ensuring data availability in case of natural disasters or accidents at any particular region.

39: What is Scale-Out approach?

Answer:

When the memory requirements go beyond a single server or to ensure high availability in cases of node failures, data is placed across a group of servers as a distributed landscape; this is scale-out approach.

40: How is the Scale-Out architecture configured in HANA environment?

Answer:

In the Scale-Out architecture where data is placed across a group of servers, N active servers and one standby server are configured for each cluster along with shared file system across all servers. During startup one server gets elected as active master. The active master assigns a volume to each starting index server or no volume in case of standby servers. This is to ensure high data availability and efficient disaster tolerance.

41: Which services will be active on each of the nodes in a scale-out landscape?

Answer:

Name server and Index server will be active on all nodes; Statistics server will be active only on the active node and only Name server will be active on the Standby node. During startup, one server in the cluster becomes the Active Master which assigns volumes to the remaining Index Servers.

42: How is Master Name server failure handled in the distributed landscape?

Answer:

If the Name server in the master node fails, another of the remaining Name-servers will become the active node.

43: How is Master Index server failure handled in the distributed landscape?

Answer:

In case of Master Index server failure, the Master Name server will detect the Index server failure and triggers the failover. During this process, the Master Name server assigns the volume to the Standby server.

44: What is the significance of XS Engine (Extended Application Service)?

Answer:

XS Engine allows web-based applications to connect to SAP HANA database; clients can fetch data through HTTP connection. This is an optional component in SAP HANA appliance.

Data Provisioning

45: What are the different replication scenarios available in SAP HANA?
Answer:
The different replication scenarios available in SAP HANA are:
  a) Log-Based
  b) Trigger-Based and
  c) ETL-Based Replication

46: What are the different types of Data Provisioning supported by SAP HANA?
Answer:
The different Data Provisioning methods supported by SAP HANA are:
  a) SAP Landscape Transformation (SLT)
  b) Business Objects Data services (BODS)
  c) Flat File Upload
  d) Direct Extractor Connection

47: Which tool provides trigger based replication services?
Answer:
SAP Landscape Transformation (SLT) supports trigger based replication into HANA.

48: What are the key benefits of SLT Replication or Trigger-Based Approach?
Answer:
The key benefits of SLT Replication are:
  a) Allows real-time data replication from SAP and NON-SAP sources, replicating only relevant data into HANA
  b) Ability to migrate data into HANA format while replicating data in real-time
  c) Extended source system release coverage from SAP ERP
  d) Leverages proven SLO technology
  e) Simple and fast set-up of LT replicator
  f) Fully integrated with SAP HANA Studio

49: When should a customer go for SLT over other replication methods?
Answer:
SAP customers should go for SLT Replication if real-time data and faster implementation is the business requirement typically for sourcing from SAP ERP systems into SAP HANA.

50: What are the technologies used by SLT Replication Server?
Answer:
The different technologies used by SLT Replication Server are:
   a) TDMS
   b) SLO and
   c) Near Zero Downtime

51: Which connection method is used between Source System and the SAP LT Replication Server?
Answer:
RFC Connection establishes the connection between the Source System and the SLT Replication Server.

52: Which connection method is used between SAP LT Replication Server and SAP HANA system?
Answer:
DB Connection establishes the connection between the SLT Replication Server and SAP HANA target system.

53: Should SAP LT Replication Server be a separate system always?
Answer:
No, SAP LT Replication Server need not be a separate system always. If the data replication load do not impact the performance of the source system, then SLT can be set up on the same server.

54: What is the prerequisite while installing SAP LT Replication Server?
Answer:

SAP LT Replication Server does not have to be a separate SAP system and can run on any SAP system with SAP NetWeaver 7.02 ABAP stack (Kernel 7.20EXT).

55: What is the recommended method of installing SAP LT Replication Server?
Answer:
Though SAP LT Replication Server does not have to be a separate SAP system, it is recommended to install the SLT Server on a separate system as high replication load would impact the performance of the source system.

56: Which technology supports real-time replication of SAP Cluster tables into HANA database?
Answer:
SAP Landscape Transformation (SLT) supports the real-time replication of SAP Cluster tables into HANA.

57: A single source system can be connected to several target schemas in SLT, what is the maximum limit?
Answer:
Currently up to 1:4 is supported in SLT replication.

58: What is the purpose of DB trigger in SLT?
Answer:
DB trigger considers only relevant table changes for DB recording and are recorded in logging tables; the replicated changes are later deleted from the logging tables. This approach will not have any performance impact in the source system.

59: What is the purpose of Controller Module in SLT?
Answer:
Controller Module ensures mapping between HANA target database structure and source system structure. It also allows conversion of data values and scheduling options while replicating the source data.

60: Which tool supports ETL based replication into HANA?
Answer:
Business Objects Data services (BODS) supports ETL based replication into SAP HANA.

61: What are the advantages of using BODS to load data into SAP HANA?
Answer:
The advantages of using BODS to load data into SAP HANA are:
- a) Loads unstructured data into SAP HANA
- b) Sorts and filters relevant business data
- c) Reads BI Content extractors or SAP function modules thereby reusing the logic
- d) Merges multiple data streams
- e) Transforms the data before loading using advanced and complex transformations
- f) Supports connectivity to a wide range of data sources

62: What are the limitations while using BODS for data replication?
Answer:
The limitations while using BODS for data replication are:
- a) Since BODS uses batch mode to load the data, real-time capabilities will be limited; only near real-time can be achieved
- b) ETL based replication takes longer time to implement

63: Which SAP ECC table stores the extractors' information used in Data Services?
Answer:
ROOSATTR table contains information on the SAP extractors used in Data Services.

64: Which file types are supported in flat file upload to SAP HANA database?
Answer:

xls, .xlsx and .csv are the supported file types that can be uploaded into SAP HANA.

65: What are the steps to follow to upload a flat file into HANA?
Answer:
The steps to upload a flat file into HANA are:
a) Choose Import ⟶ SAP HANA Content ⟶ Data from Local File
b) Select the source file to upload
c) Select the target table where data should be imported (new or existing)
d) Manage table definition and do the mapping of source to target columns
e) Select finish and go to preview the target table

66: Which are the two options available for target table during flat file upload?
Answer:
The two options available for target table during flat file upload are:
a) **New:** On selecting New, a new table will be created in the HANA database with the entered name under the specified schema.
b) **Existing:** On selecting Existing, data will be appended to an existing table in HANA.

67: Which is the most relevant control tables involved in SLT replication?
Answer:
RS_ORDER and RS_STATUS are the significant control tables used in SLT replication.

68: What are the parameters required to configure SLT for replicating SAP data into HANA database?
Answer:
The parameters required while configuring SLT are:

a) Connection to Source System (SAP or Non-SAP, RFC Destination, Allow Multiple Usage, Read from Single Client)
b) Connection to HANA System (Username, Password, Hostname, Instance Number)
c) Table space Assignment
d) Replication Options

69: What are the scheduling options available while configuring SLT?
Answer:
The different scheduling options available while configuring SLT are:
a) Real-Time
b) Schedule by Time and
c) Schedule by Interval

70: In the data replication options, what is the difference between Stop and Suspend Replication?
Answer:
In Stop mode, the SLT server will stop the delta recording for the tables and delete the DB trigger.
While in Suspend mode, the replication will be stopped but DB recording will be kept active. Hence the replication process can be resumed without repeating the initial load.

71: What are the types of Transformation Rules available in SLT replication?
Answer:
The types of Transformation Rules available in SLT replication are:
a) Parameter-based rules and
b) Event-based rules

72: Which replication method uses ODP (Operational Data Provider) for data replication?

Answer:
Business Objects Data services 4.0 supports ODP for data replication.

73: What are the benefits of ODP in Data Services?
Answer:
The benefits of ODP in Data Services are:
  a) Access to all Business Suite Extractors without going through SAP BW
  b) Both initial and delta data capture
  c) Stream data from SAP to BODS without any staging area

74: Which transaction is used for releasing extractors specified by the customers?
Answer:
RODPS_OS_EXPOSE transaction releases the extractors specified by the customers.

75: What are the different methods in Data Services for extracting data from SAP applications?
Answer:
The different methods in Data Services for extracting SAP data are:
  a) RFC_READ_TABLE
  b) Read tables via ABAP dataflows
  c) RFC/BAPI function calls and
  d) IDOCs

76: Which dataflow in BODS is used to extract large volumes of data from SAP ECC?
Answer:
ABAP dataflows should be used to extract large volumes of data from SAP ECC; it pushes the join operations to the SAP application and hence gives better performance while reading multiple ECC tables.

Modeling

77: What are the credentials you need to add a system to SAP HANA Studio?

Answer:

The credentials needed to add a system to SAP HANA Studio are:

   a) Hostname
   b) Instance Number
   c) User name and
   d) Password

78: Which all folders do you see after logging into HANA Studio?

Answer:

The different folders visible after logging into HANA Studio are:

   a) Catalog,
   b) Content and
   c) Security

79: Do the information models store data in SAP HANA?

Answer:

No, only the physical tables store data within SAP HANA.

80: How does HANA minimize data duplication?

Answer:

Within HANA, only the physical tables are replicated to store data. The information models built in the modeler will create views which do not store any data; it will fetch the data from the tables during runtime. Hence SAP HANA eliminates data duplication and no materialized aggregates are created.

81: What are perspectives in HANA Studio and how are they relevant?

Answer:

Perspectives are predefined views or user interfaces for HANA Studio users.

The Modeler Perspective is used by Data Architects to build information models. The Administration Console is mainly used by administrators to administrate and monitor the HANA engine.

82: Which perspective should you select to create data models in HANA?
Answer:
Modeler Perspective should be selected to create data models in HANA.

83: How will you change the connection to another HANA system within Studio?
Answer:
If you want to change the current connection to another system, go to Quick launch -> Select System -> Choose Connection.

84: What are the different types of views that you deal with in SAP HANA modeling?
Answer:
The different types of views in SAP HANA modeling are:
   a) Attribute Views
   b) Analytic Views and
   c) Calculation Views

85: What is an Attribute View? Brief on.
Answer:
Attribute views are reusable dimensions or master data objects. Attributes Views can have single or multiple tables and are reusable objects. E.g. Time, Product.
In the star schema of an analytic view, the attribute view is shown as a single dimension table (although it might join multiple tables), that is joined to the fact table.

86: What is an Analytic View? Brief on.
Answer:
Analytic view is a cube-like view by joining attributes view to the fact data; it is used to model data that includes measures.
An analytic view would have a Data Foundation layer based on a

transactional table and attribute views are joined to the data foundation to make it look like a star schema model.

87: What is a Calculation View? Brief on.
Answer:
The highest and most advanced information model in SAP HANA is a Calculation View. It comes into picture when measures from more than one fact table are involved in the business case or advanced logic is required that cannot be handled in attribute or analytic views.
Calculation views can have complex calculation logic, advanced SQLs, include schema tables, attribute views or analytic views, etc.

88: What are the types of Attribute Views?
Answer:
The two types of Attribute Views are:
  a) Standard and
  b) Time

89: What are the types of Calculation Views?
Answer:
The two types of Calculation Views are:
  a) Graphical and
  b) Script

90: While creating an Attribute View, you will have options as 'Standard and 'Derived', what is the difference between the two?
Answer:
Standard view is typically used for creating a new Attribute View. Derived view is created as a reference to the base view; it would always be read only. In some business cases, it might be required to use the same attribute view more than once with different join types in an analytic view. In such cases, one can create a derived attribute view using the base view which acts as a reference to the same.

91: What are the properties of a derived attribute view?
Answer:
a) The derived view will always be opened in the read only mode; the only editable field will be its description.
b) The derived view will always reference its base attribute view; any changes to the base view will get reflected in the derived view as well.

92: The Script Based Calculation View can be written in two ways, what are they?
Answer:
The Script Based Calculation View can be written using SQL Script and CE functions.

93: What is mandatory in an Attribute View without which you cannot activate it?
Answer:
It is mandatory to choose at least one key attribute for the attribute view.

94: What is mandatory in an Analytic View without which you cannot activate it?
Answer:
It is mandatory to choose at least one measure for the analytic view.

95: What are the conditions to follow while selecting measures in an Analytic View?
Answer:
Measures that are selected for inclusion in an analytic view must all point to the same table.

96: SAP HANA appliance comes with different types of engines, what are they?
Answer:
a) Join Engine

The Join Engine is used to perform all type of joins
b) OLAP Engine
The OLAP Engine is used for calculation and aggregation
c) Calculation Engine
The Calculation Engine is used on top of OLAP engine or Join Engine for complex calculations which cannot be done by Join Engine or OLAP Engine

97: Where do the information models get created in HANA?
Answer:
The information models or column views are always located in _SYS_BIC schema.

98: How will you query data from the information models in HANA?
Answer:
Once you activate the models in HANA, it creates column views under _SYS_BIC schema. To query data from the same, you can write a standard SQL in the SQL editor as
select from
"SYS_BIC"."<package name>/<view name>".

99: Which schema holds the metadata information in SAP HANA?
Answer:
Schema _SYS_BI holds all the metadata information in SAP HANA.

100: What are the different ways to preview data in an information view?
Answer:
Data Preview and SQL Editor are the two ways to preview data in an information view.

101: What options do you get while doing Data Preview?
Answer:

Data Preview gives the following options for data analysis:
   a) **Raw Data:** Returns the complete data results of the information model
   b) **Distinct Values:** Returns the unique or distinct values of the attributes in the view
   c) **Analysis:** Allows drag and drop analysis of the data using charts, tables and filters

102: List the different types of Joins available in SAP HANA.
Answer:
The different join types available in SAP HANA are:
   a) Inner
   b) Left Outer
   c) Right Outer
   d) Text Join
   e) Referential

103: What should you be aware of while using Inner Joins?
Answer:
Inner joins should be used with caution because of the following reasons:
   a) Facts without any dimension and dimensions without any fact will be excluded
   b) Join will be always executed giving negative performance implications

104: Which are the fastest and slowest joins in SAP HANA context?
Answer:
From a performance perspective, the Left Outer Join and Referential Join are equally fast depending on the data, while the Inner Join is comparatively slower.

105: What is a Referential Join? Explain.
Answer:
Referential Join is a newly introduced join in SAP HANA

environment. It is an optimized and faster join which behaves according to the data selection criteria, where join will be executed only when attributes from both the tables are selected. It acts as Inner Join if fields are selected from both the tables, while as Left Outer Join in case no fields are selected from the right table.

106: Why should Referential Joins be used with caution?
Answer:
Referential joins come with a warning. They can be used only when the referential integrity is ensured, that is, for each row in left table, there should be at least one related record in the right table. So unless the data integrity is guaranteed, you shouldn't be using referential joins, it can give unexpected results in such cases. Also if there is a filter on the right table, referential joins cannot be used.

107: Right outer join is rarely used, give a business case where Right Outer Join would be used.
Answer:
Right Outer join returns all the rows from the right table (dimension), even if there are no matches in the left table (fact). For example, Sales fact is joined with Material dimension using Right Outer join. If you want to report on the materials for which Sales have not happened for a period of time, the blank entries of the Sales fact can be queried.

108: What are the join properties to be defined while connecting two tables?
Answer:
The join properties to be defined while connecting two tables are:
  a) Right and Left Elements
  b) Join Type
  c) Cardinality
  d) Language Column (for text join)

109: Define Cardinality and its different types.
Answer:
Cardinality refers to the maximum number of times a record in one table can be associated with related records in another table. In general, cardinalities can be 1:1, N:1, 1:N and N:M.

110: Explain about Text Join in SAP HANA.
Answer:
Text Joins are used to join text tables with master data tables and can only be used with SAP tables where the language column (SPRAS) is present.
For each attribute it is possible to define a description mapping that will be specific to the end users' language. In text join, user language will be used as a filter at runtime to find the right translation for that attribute.

111: Give a SAP example where you can use Text Join.
Answer:
The join between MARA to MAKT can be Text Join. Language column would be MAKT.SPRAS.

112: What are the best practices to be followed while connecting tables in HANA?
Answer:
The best practices to be followed while connecting tables in HANA are:
  a) Always use Left Outer join with cardinality N:1 from fact to dimension, as a general rule
  b) The cardinality must be decreased going from the center of the star schema to the outside, that is, only N:1 or 1:1 joins are advised going from the fact table to the dimension
  c) Drag Join lines from the fact table to the outer tables, and then change the cardinality

113: Mention few cases where activating the analytic model

would result in error.
Answer:
Below are few cases violating which can give error in your
analytic models:
  a) If the join from data foundation to an attribute view is a
      multi column join, all the attributes in the join condition
      must point to the same table.
  b) In the link between the fact table to an attribute view, a
      table must not appear twice in the join path.

114: Is self joins possible in SAP HANA?
Answer:
Yes, you can have self-joins in SAP HANA, i.e. several instances of
the same table in an attribute view. But it will give you error when
this attribute view is used in an analytic view.

**115: How will you resolve the "self join detected on table" error
in an analytic view?**
Answer:
The self join error is generated when same table is detected twice
in the join path between the fact table and an attribute view. An
attribute view with self joins will give you error only when used
in an analytic view. In such a case, you would need to modify the
model to eliminate one instance of the table from the join path
either by moving this to a new attribute view or by pushing the
join logic to calculation view.

**116: Why is it advised to ensure decreasing cardinality going
from the center of the star schema to the outside?**
Answer:
If cardinality increases going outward, say 1:N or N:M, it might
lead to unexpected multiplication of fact table rows. You will also
get a warning message during the model deployment.

**117: Briefly mention the steps involved in creating a simple
Analytic View.**

Answer:

The steps involved in creating an Analytic View are listed below:

  a) Right click on a package -> New -> Analytic View -> Define the name, description and view type -> Ok
  b) You will see Data foundation, Logical join and Semantics
  c) In Data Foundation, the fact tables should be added and attributes/measures be selected from the same. The measures should all come from the central table
  d) In Logical join, the fact table or data foundation should be joined to the relevant attribute views to make it look like a star schema model
  e) Semantics will show the output structure of the model

118: Which folder cannot be accessed from the Administrator Console?

Answer:

Content folder cannot be accessed from the Administrator Console perspective.

119: What are the different types of objects under a package?

Answer:

The different types of objects that come under a package are Package (sub package), Attribute View, Analytic View, Calculation View, Analytic Privilege, Procedure and Decision Tables.

120: Which calendars can be created using Time Attribute views?

Answer:

Gregorian and Fiscal calendars can be created using Time Attribute views.

121: What are the different components in a Graphical Calculation view?

Answer:

The different components in a Graphical Calculation View are

Projection, Union, Join and Aggregation.

122: How is Currency Conversion supported in HANA?
Answer:
Currency Conversion is supported only in Analytic Views and Script Based Calculation Views.

123: Which is the preferred way of doing Currency Conversion?
Answer:
The preferred way to do currency conversion for measures is to model in an Analytic View.

124: What is the prerequisite to enable the currency conversion functionality?
Answer:
Few of the TCUR* tables in SAP must be replicated into HANA for currency conversions to work correctly (TCURR, TCURV, TCURF, TCURN, TCURX).

125: Which transaction code is used to get the table relationships in SAP ERP?
Answer:
SD11 transaction code returns the table relationships in SAP ERP.

126: What are the cons of using Inner Join in information models?
Answer:
Inner Join gives the slowest performance as the join will always be executed irrespective of the fields queried. In case of inner join between fact and dimension, you will lose the facts with fragmented dimensions in the result set due to missing corresponding dimension entry.

127: In which scenarios can Inner Join give better performance?
Answer:
If you have filters defined in either or both tables in an

information model, Inner Joins can be faster as it will reduce the number of records involved in the join.

128: If there are filters and joins included in a view, how does the query get executed on the same?
Answer:
During the query runtime, filters are first applied to the tables before the join is executed, hence smaller data sets would be involved in the join.

129: What is Full Outer Join and how is it supported in SAP HANA?
Answer:
Full Outer Join is both Left Outer and Right Outer joins combined; it returns all the rows from both the tables in the join irrespective of the matching columns. For non-matching rows, nulls will be returned for the respective fields from both tables.
SAP HANA does not support Full Outer Join.

130: Which join property is defined only for Text Joins while connecting tables?
Answer:
Language Column is specified only for Text Joins while connecting tables.

131: What are Temporal Joins?
Answer:
Temporal Joins are non-equi joins. They are used to filter out the records based on time interval between the fact and the master data, that is, include or exclude the fact data depending on the date fields while executing the join.
For Example, SALES_DATE between FROM_DATE and TO_DATE.

132: How do you create a Temporal Join in an information model?

Answer:
To create a Temporal Join between data foundation and attribute view, you have to define the same in the join properties. Temporal Column, From Column, To Column and Temporal Condition need to be entered in the join properties. Temporal Column must be in the fact table and, the To and From Columns in the attribute view. Defining these properties will allow you to create a temporal join in the information model.

133: What are the limitations of Temporal Join in HANA?
Answer:
The limitations of Temporal Join are:
   a) Supported only in Logical View and SQL Based Calculation View
   b) Join type should be Referential Join
   c) Data types supported are timestamp, date, and integer

134: Is Temporal Join supported by all versions of SAP HANA?
Answer:
No, Temporal Join is supported only from SP05 and onwards.

135: In Script Based Calculation Views what is recommended to be used, the built in functions or SQL?
Answer:
It is recommended to use the built in functions over SQL in script based calculation views as CE functions are well optimized and give better performance through parallel processing by the calculation engine.
Also SQL is less optimized; it can fetch more fields than what is requested.

136: Out of Union and Join, which is preferred in a Calculation View?
Answer:
Union is always preferred in a calculation view, because join in Calculation View will lead to bad performance implications as the

calculation engine is not optimized for the same. The join will be done in the Join engine causing data transfer between the calculation and join engines, thereby degrading the performance.

137: In which view should joins be implemented to get better performance?
Answer:
Always prefer to join tables in the Attribute View or Analytic View. Joins are well optimized in the Join Engine; hence they are faster than joins in the Calculation Engine.

138: Which is the best place to create calculated attributes?
Answer:
The best place to create calculated attributes is Calculation Views as it runs in the calculation engine where the calculation logic is processed. Since there is no data transfer in this case, performance would be better. Creating calculated attributes in Analytic View or Attribute view must be avoided as Join/OLAP engine is not optimized for the same. The desired calculation will be done in the calculation engine and result set transferred back to Join/OLAP engine, data transfer between the engines would impact the performance.

139: Where can the UNION function be realized in HANA?
Answer:
Unions are not supported in Attribute Views or Analytic Views and can be realized only in Calculation Views.

140: How will you combine multiple Analytic Views without impacting the performance of your query?
Answer:
Multiple Analytic Views can be combined using Union with Constant values without impacting the performance.

141: How is Union with Constant values different from Standard Union?

Answer:
Standard Union simply combines the two data sets while in Union with Constant values mapping is done a bit differently. The uncommon attributes or measures from the two data sources are mapped in such a way that they come in a single row and the unmapped columns for a particular source can be assigned any constant value.

142: What is the main difference between UNION in graphical view and CE_UNION_ALL function in Script Based Calculation View?
Answer:
The UNION function in graphical view can accept 1 to N input sources whereas CE_UNION_ALL function can accept only two input sources at a time.

143: What are the advantages of Graphical Calculation View over Script Based Calculation View?
Answer:
The advantages of Graphical Calculation View over Script Based view are:
- a) Easy to build
- b) No SQL coding required
- c) Union with Constant values supported
- d) Union allows N input sources
- e) Fetches only the selected fields

144: How do you create copies of an existing model?
Answer:
There are two ways of creating copies of an existing model:
Create a new object as 'Copy From' an existing view.
Alternatively, right click on an object and select 'Copy'; go to the desired target location and select 'Paste'.

145: What is the Refactor option available for a view?
Answer:

Refactor functionality is used to move views and packages to different target folders; it is like cut and paste.

146: What are the different types of measures in HANA?
Answer:
The three types of measures supported by HANA are Standard Measures, Calculated Measures and Restricted Measures.

147: What are Restricted Columns?
Answer:
Restricted Columns or Measures are a subset of the original measure, restricted based on some attribute.

For example, there are Country and Amount columns in a table; and a restricted measure is created on Country. The output will show different country names as columns and the total amounts against each as the data.

148: How will you to create a Restricted Column in an Attribute View?
Answer:
Restricted Columns are supported only in Analytic views and not in Attribute or Calculation Views.

149: How do you create stand alone Text Tables in an Attribute View?
Answer:
In some cases, the text table is not joined to any other table but you will still need the dynamic language texts. Create an attribute view with the text table and define a dynamic filter on the language columns as $$language$$, this will support multilingual texts.

150: Are Hierarchies supported in SAP HANA?
Answer:
Yes, we can create two types of Hierarchies – Level Hierarchy and Parent Child Hierarchy.

151: How are the two Hierarchy types different?
Answer:
a) **Level Hierarchies** are inflexible in nature and can be accessed only in defined order; members of this hierarchy can be of same or different types and can be at a single level. Time hierarchy is an example that can be drilled down to Year, Quarter, Month, etc.
b) **Parent Child Hierarchies** have members of the same type and are more flexible. Typical example is Employee and Manager.

152: What are the key points to remember while creating a Hierarchy in HANA?
Answer:
While creating a Hierarchy in HANA, it is important to consider the below points.
a) Set the child attribute's property 'Principal Key' to True.
b) Set 'Hierarchy Active' to True for all non-key attributes that need to be reported via MDX (MDX shows only key attributes by default).

153: Where do you define Hierarchies in HANA Studio?
Answer:
Only Attribute View supports Hierarchies in HANA.

154: How can you enforce calculations at each line item before aggregation of Measures?
Answer:
While defining the calculated columns, select the option "Calculate Before Aggregation" to enforce the calculations to be done at the line item level.

155: What content does the Auto Documentation include and in which format?
Answer:
SAP HANA generates the auto document in pdf format. The

document includes details about the view, package, attributes details like description, data type and source column details and join properties like join type, cardinality, left and right tables and language column. Filters are not captured in the auto document.

156: In which scenario will you build a calculation view with SQL script rather than the graphical one?
Answer:
Calculation view with SQL script would be preferred, if the business case is:
   a) To use standard SQL functions which are not available within the modeler
   b) To create and use custom reusable calculation functions

157: Which component breaks the SQL query into executable parts?
Answer:
SQL parser breaks the SQL query into executable parts.

158: What is the functionality of SQL Optimizer?
Answer:
SQL Optimizer decides the best way to execute the information models and queries by calling the relevant processing engines. It typically creates the execution plan for the user query.

159: Describe few best practices while creating Script Based Calculation Views.
Answer:
Few best practices to be followed while creating Script Based Calculation Views are:
   a) In Calculation Views, do not mix SQL and CE Functions within the same script
   b) Preferably use CE Functions as they are well optimized and parallelized

160: How does mixing of SQL and CE operators impact the

performance?

Answer:

Mixing of SQL and CE operators degrades the calculation view performance, as it hits different processing engines and data transfer between the engines can cost you time.

161: What are the different ways to filter data at the lower layers while modeling?

Answer:

By using Filters, WHERE clause, Analytic Privilege and Input Parameters, data can be filtered out in the information models.

162: How are Filters different from WHERE clause?

Answer:

Filters get applied first before the query execution starts, but WHERE clause reduces the data set by applying the filter on the results of a query. Hence filters are faster as the data set is reduced before the query execution plan or join.

163: Is it possible to create dynamic filters in an information model?

Answer:

Yes, using Variables and Input Parameters dynamic filters can be created in an information model.

164: What is the difference between Variables and Input Parameters?

Answer:

Variables are defined to pass runtime filters into the model from the application layer. These are created and applied to the attributes as a filter to enable data restriction. They can only take values of the related attribute.

An Input Parameter can be used to process a calculation based on the user input. It can be any value the user wants to enter or select.

165: Describe the different Table Types available in HANA.

Answer:

The different table types available in HANA are:

a) **Column:** Column stores tables preferred for querying large number of records with few selected attributes

b) **Row:** Row stores tables preferred for querying fewer records with all the attributes selected

c) **History Column:** Support time travel for querying against historic states of the database

d) **Global Temporary:** Table definition available globally while data visible only to the current session and

e) **Local Temporary:** Table definition and data visible only to the current session

166: What is the significance of History Column table?

Answer:

History Column table supports time travel; the history instances of the database can be queried. In such tables, any update or delete will result in a new record to be populated with the original record being turned inactive.

167: How do you query from a History Table to get time travelled data?

Answer:

You can query a History Column table to fetch history data snapshot using commit id or timestamp as

SELECT <list> FROM <table> AS OF [COMMIT ID I TIMESTAMP] <commit_id> I <timestamp>

168: Procedures are created using executable rights, what are the two types of rights?

Answer:

The two types of rights while creating a Procedure are Invoker's Rights and Definer's Rights.

169: How is the Definer mode different from Invoker mode in procedures?

Answer:

In "definer" mode, the procedure is executed with the privileges of the definer of the procedure.

In "invoker" mode, execution of the procedure is performed with the privileges of the caller of the function.

170: How can you preview the data results of a Procedure?
Answer:

Data results of a Procedure can be retrieved using CALL function by a client or other supported front end interfaces; one procedure can also be called by another procedure.

171: What are the different CE functions used to read data from an information model?
Answer:

CE_COLUMN_TABLE, CE_JOIN_VIEW, CE_OLAP_VIEW and CE_CALC_VIEW are the select or read functions available in HANA.

172: What are the failure modes available in Currency Conversion?
Answer:

The different failure modes available in Currency Conversion are Fail, Set to NULL and Ignore.

173: What are the prerequisites to enable user prompt for target currency in Currency Conversion?
Answer:

The user prompt variable defined should be of type Currency, data type VARCHAR and length 5.

174: How is Currency Conversion done in Calculation Views?
Answer:

Currency Conversion is supported only in Scripts Based Calculation View; it is performed by using CE_CONVERSION function.

175: What is Fuzzy Search and how is it supported in HANA?
Answer:
Fuzzy Search enables fetching of strings or texts from the HANA database that approximately matches a pattern rather than exactly. Python based scripts support this text analytics on large and unstructured data columns. Fulltext Search and Text Analysis in HANA allow you to use this functionality.

176: Which data types does Fuzzy Search support?
Answer:
Fuzzy Search is supported only in TEXT, SHORTTEXT, VARCHAR, NVARCHAR and DATE data types.

177: How does HANA speed up the fuzzy search functionality?
Answer:
To speed up the fuzzy search, the full text indexes or fast fuzzy search structures are enabled for the required columns, especially the ones used in performance critical queries.

178: What is the relevance of Fuzzy Score?
Answer:
Fuzzy Score gives an indication of the similarity between the strings compared. The score gets calculated between 0.0 and 1.0 on comparison; higher the score, the more similar the strings are.

179: How is fuzzy search realized using SQL query?
Answer:
By using CONTAINS function in the WHERE clause, you can call the fuzzy search in the SQL query. The SCORE function in SELECT statement returns the Fuzzy Score of the columns used. The SQL query format would be as
SELECT SCORE() AS score, * FROM documents
WHERE CONTAINS (doc_content, 'text', FUZZY (0.6)) ORDER BY score DESC;

180: How will you check the model dependencies while

changing or deleting information objects?
Answer:
Using Where-Used List, it is possible to check the references where an information object is used; this could be helpful to know the impact of changes done in the data model. Do a right click on any object and select "Where-Used" function to find the dependencies.

181: Is versioning of models possible in HANA?
Answer:
It is possible to get the version history of Information Models by using History option; do a right click on any object and select the "History" function. Version, Name of the user and Activation Date are available in the Version History.

182: What is a Delivery Unit and how is it relevant?
Answer:
Delivery Unit is typically used for transporting information models, it is used to group the transportable objects as a single unit for content delivery and to export from source to target server.

183: How many types of Import/Export are possible in HANA?
Answer:
The two types of import/export possible in HANA are Client-Side and Server-Side.

184: How is Client-Side Import different from Server-Side Import of information models?
Answer:
Importing objects using Delivery Units is called Server-Side Import; this function will import grouped objects or delivery unit from the server location available in .tgz format.
Importing objects using Developer Mode is called Client-Side Import; this function will import individual objects from client location to your SAP HANA modeler.

Server-Side import does automatic activation of the imported models and can overwrite entire packages, but Client-Side import does not activate the objects.

185: What is the significance of Life Cycle Management in SAP HANA?

Answer:

Life Cycle Management contains information about Upgrade/Updates on SAP HANA and details on the current version installed by setting up a connection to the SAP Marketplace.

186: What are the steps involved to implement SAP HANA appliance?

Answer:

The sequence of steps to implement SAP HANA appliance are:

a) **SAP HANA system setup:** Install and setup the SAP HANA server

b) **Data Provisioning:** Replicate the source data into the HANA database

c) **Modeling:** Design and build the information models and

d) **Reporting:** Consume the models for user reporting

187: How is the SAP delivered content Information model accessed?

Answer:

Mass Copy functionality lets you access the SAP delivered content.

188: What is the relevance of Schema Mapping?

Answer:

Schema Mapping is used when the schema in source system is not same as the schema in target system. By mapping the logical schemas with the physical schemas, it will point to the respective schemas while transferring information objects from a source system to target. It is significant while transporting the models from development to testing and to production.

Security and Authorization

189: What are the different types of privileges in SAP HANA?
Answer:
The different types of privileges in SAP HANA are:
   a) System Privileges
   b) SQL Privileges
   c) Package Privileges
   d) Analytic Privileges

190: What is the privilege required to access data from the activated views?
Answer:
_SYS_REPO must have SELECT WITH GRANT OPTION privilege for all the schemas used in the models, else you will not be able to access data from the activated views.

191: Which Authentication Methods are supported by SAP HANA?
Answer:
The four authentication methods currently supported in HANA are User / Password, Kerberos, SAML and X509.

192: What are the steps involved in managing users and roles in Security?
Answer:
Following steps are involved while managing users and roles in HANA Security:
   a) Define and create Roles
   b) Assign privileges to Roles
   c) Create Users
   d) Grant Roles to User

193: Which single-sign-on (SSO) authentication method is supported by SAP HANA?
Answer:
Kerberos is the SSO authentication method supported by SAP HANA.

194: Which pre-delivered role with vital privileges is assigned to the system administrator in SAP HANA?
Answer:
CONTENT_ADMIN is the vital role assigned to the SAP HANA system administrator.

This page is intentionally left blank

Reporting

195: Which are the reporting tools supported by HANA?
Answer:
The different reporting tools supported by HANA are:
  a) Microsoft Excel
  b) SAP Business Objects BI 4.0
  c) Analysis Office
  d) Analysis OLAP, Explorer
  e) Crystal Reports
  f) Dashboards and
  e) Web Intelligence

196: Which database clients are available to connect to SAP HANA?
Answer:
ODBC, JDBC, ODBO and SQL DBC are the database clients that can connect to HANA.

197: Which web-based interfaces support HANA connectivity?
Answer:
OData, XMLA and JavaScript are the web-interfaces that can connect to HANA.

198: Which connectivity methods support reporting off HANA?
Answer:
SQL, MDX and BICS connectivity supports reporting off HANA.

199: Which drivers connect to HANA database via SQL?
Answer:
ODBC and JDBC are the drivers that connect via SQL to the HANA database.

200: Which driver uses MDX Connectivity to HANA?
Answer:
ODBO driver connects via MDX to the HANA database.

201: How do BICS drivers connect to HANA?

Answer:
BICS database requests are made via SQL DBC to the HANA database.

202: Which reporting tools use ODBC or JDBC driver connectivity?
Answer:
Crystal Reports (2011 and Enterprise), Dashboards, Web Intelligence, Explorer and Business Objects IDT (Semantic Layer) use ODBC or JDBC driver connectivity while reporting.

203: Which reporting tools use ODBO driver connectivity?
Answer:
Microsoft Excel uses ODBO driver connectivity while reporting.

204: Which reporting tools use SQL DBC driver or BICS?
Answer:
Analysis Office and Analysis OLAP use BICS connectivity while reporting.

205: Which tool is used to create BI Universes for Reporting?
Answer:
Information Design Tool (IDT) is used for creating BI Universes for reporting.

206: Which Connectivity supports Hierarchies in SAP HANA models?
Answer:
Only MDX connectivity or Excel supports Hierarchies in SAP HANA models.

207: In which scenario will users go for reporting in MS Excel?
Answer:
Multidimensional reporting (cross-tab) is supported only via MS Excel; it is also preferable for quick and easy data reporting. But Excel would be available only locally and hence subjected to

desktop performance limitations.

208: What is the significance of Crystal Reports?
Answer:
Crystal Reports are used in business cases which require corporate data in highly formatted and aligned manner for further analysis and greater insight. These reports are automated and pixel perfect reports used for global deployments.

209: What is the significance of Dashboards?
Answer:
Dashboards allow business users to visualize data in the most attractive and personalized way; it has powerful analysis options with sliders and other controls, drill-downs, maps, charts, gauges, etc. for effective decision making.

210: Which reporting tool allows ad hoc reporting and interacts with information?
Answer:
Web Intelligence allows ad-hoc reporting and interacts with information.

211: What are the advantages of Webi reporting?
Answer:
The main advantages of Webi reporting are:
  a) Powerful and easy to use reports
  b) Business users can extend an existing report for detailed analysis
  c) Business users can start from a blank template for any queries or statistics
  d) Filtering, sorting, calculations, etc. support information interactivity

212: Which reporting tool allows complex reporting on historical data to determine trends and make forecasts?
Answer:

Analysis for Office and OLAP allows complex reporting on historical data for trends and forecasts.

213: What are the advantages of reporting through BI Explorer?
Answer:
   a) Explorer supports quick and immediate answers to business questions searching directly on the pre-indexed data.
   b) Fast search across volumes of data anywhere, simple and spontaneous data visualization, heterogeneous data sources adds to its functionalities.
   c) It searches across all data sources like BI universes, SAP BWA sources or HANA systems.
   d) Analysis can be easily shared with others as CSV or image or by sending the link by email.

214: What are the mandatory steps to be followed to use Explorer with SAP HANA for reporting?
Answer:
The steps to be followed while using Explorer for SAP HANA reporting are:
   a) Create an Information Space in Explorer
   b) Index the Explorer Information Space
   c) Configure the Explorer in Central Management Console

215: Which reporting tools connect through BI Universe to SAP HANA?
Answer:
Explorer, Crystal Reports, Dashboards and Web Intelligence are the reporting tools that connect through BI Universes to SAP HANA.

216: What are the steps involved in creating a Universe through IDT?
Answer:
While creating a Universe though IDT, the following steps are

involved:
a) Create a new project
b) Establish a Relational Connection to SAP HANA server (hostname, instance, username, password, authentication mode, etc.)
c) Select the driver as ODBC or JDBC
d) Create a Data Foundation (single or multisource)
e) Create the Business Layer on top of the Data Foundation
f) Define the dimensions, measures, aggregates, etc. in the Business Layer
g) Publish the Connection and Business Layer

217: What are the objects accessible while creating an IDT Data Foundation?
Answer:
The SAP HANA objects that are accessible while creating an IDT Data Foundation are:
a) Tables and Views from the respective schemas
b) Column Views from _SYS_BIC schema

218: What is the purpose of SAP HANA Information Composer?
Answer:
SAP HANA Information Composer is a web based application that allows uploading data into the HANA database and performing simple data manipulations. Different sources like Information models or flat files can be selected as source data, combined and published for further analytics.

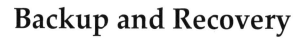

Backup and Recovery

219: Which database concept will be violated by in-memory in SAP HANA?

Answer:

Out of the four, atomicity, consistency, isolation, and durability (ACID) that guarantees database reliability, durability is the criteria that cannot be met by storing data in main memory alone. Main memory is a volatile storage; hence it loses its content when the power goes off. So the durability concept is violated by in-memory in SAP HANA.

220: How does SAP HANA ensure data reliability using in-memory?

Answer:

SAP HANA uses a persistent storage which is non-volatile, such as hard drives, SSD, or Flash devices writing data to this persistent layer in regular intervals. Hence even if the in-memory content is cleared during an outage or power failure, data is backed up in the non-volatile storage ensuring data reliability.

221: What is the significance of the persistence layer in SAP HANA?

Answer:

a) Main memory is volatile and data would be lost during a restart or power outage, hence a persistent storage is required

b) Backup and restore is available in the persistence layer

c) It ensures that changes are durable and database can be restored to the most recent state after restart

Hence the persistence layer in SAP HANA ensures data reliability and recovery during system outages

222: Which are the components in the persistence layer?

Answer:

Page Management and Logger are the components that constitute the persistence layer.

223: Which are the components in the disk storage layer?
Answer:
Data Volumes and Log Volumes are the components that constitute the disk storage layer.

224: What are redo and undo logs?
Answer:
Data pages and before images are undo logs (uncommitted transactions) that are written on to the data volumes. After images are redo logs (committed transactions) that are written on to the log volumes.

225: How does the persistence layer work in SAP HANA?
Answer:
Any changes or updates to the data are regularly marked and written to a non-volatile storage in an asynchronous manner in default intervals of 5 minutes. These changed pages are stored in save points.
Additionally the transaction log on each committed transaction is written synchronously to the non-volatile storage. This ensures that the database transactions are persistent and retrievable.

226: What are the recovery steps to follow after reboot or power failure which deletes in-memory data?
Answer:
The database pages are reloaded from the save points and then the logs are applied for the changes not included in the save points. The recovery steps to be followed are:
  a) Reload the last save point
  b) Read the uncommitted transactions saved with last save point from the Undo logs
  c) Read the committed transactions since last save point from the Redo logs

227: What are the prerequisites to restore the SAP HANA system after restart?

Answer:
The prerequisites to restore the SAP HANA system after restart are the availability of
   a) Last data save point
   b) Log between the last data save point and the time of failure

228: What are the different kinds of backup in SAP HANA?
Answer:
Data backup, Log backup and Configuration backup are the different types of backup available in SAP HANA.

229: What is the system prerequisite for backup and recovery?
Answer:
The number of hosts and physical layout of both the source and target database should be same for backup and recovery.

230: In which scenario do we need backup and recovery?
Answer:
Backup and recovery would be required in cases of disk failure or damaged data volumes.

231: What is the procedure followed for database copy using backups?
Answer:
The steps involved in database copy using backups are:
   a) Create the new target database
   b) Copy the required backups to the target folder
   c) Recover the target database to the desired point in time

232: What are the different data sources involved in the recovery process?
Answer:
The data sources involved in the recovery process are:
   a) Data backups stored in the file system
   b) Log backups stored in the file system and

c) Online logs

233: What are the steps to follow during recovery to last committed state?

Answer:

The data backups, log backups and the log area are used during the recovery process. After successfully recovering the data backup, the log entries from the log backups and the log area are automatically replayed. The steps to be followed during the recovery process are:

  a) Import save point data from data backup files into database
  b) Restart database from restored save point
  c) Replay log from log backup files and online log

234: What are the different recovery scenarios available in HANA?

Answer:

The three recovery scenarios available in SAP HANA are:

  a) Restore to last data backup state
  b) Restore to last committed state
  c) Point-in-time recovery

235: What is point-in-time recovery?

Answer:

SAP HANA allows database recovery to any point in time as requested by the user or to a specified position in the log; this is point-in-time recovery.

236: How is point-in-time recovery done in HANA, recovery to state of database at time t1?

Answer:

The steps involved in point-in-time recovery to time t1 are:

  a) Import save point data from data backup files into database from time t0 (t0 < t1)
  b) Restart database from restored save point

c) Replay log from log backup files for time between t0 and t1 and online log until the desired point in time

237: If the log area is damaged, to which state can the system be recovered?
Answer:
If the log area is damaged, the system can be restored to the last data backup state, any changes made after the most recent backup will be lost.

238: During the database recovery process, will the SAP HANA system be available?
Answer:
The SAP HANA database needs to be shut down during the recovery process, hence will be unavailable to the end users. Also, if a recovery fails in between, it must be repeated from the start.

Pricing and Licensing

239: How is the SAP HANA appliance priced?

Answer:

The volume of data and the number of users are the two pricing variables for SAP HANA. Further, different software editions are made available in SAP HANA to allow flexibility and specific customer choices based on their needs and preferences.

240: Give a brief on SAP HANA sizing.

Answer:

Sizing plays a key role in SAP HANA to calculate the right sizing of the server based on the client requirement. The amount of memory and the CPU processing power are calculated during the sizing exercise. SAP has defined the different configurations for SAP HANA as T-shirt sizes.

241: Why is the concept of T-shirt sizes significant in SAP HANA?

Answer:

SAP has defined T-shirt sizes for HANA to confine the number of hardware configurations and simplify the sizing exercise. It is according to these T-shirt sizes the hardware configurations are delivered by the SAP's partners. The server sizes need to be selected appropriately for optimal performance of the SAP HANA database. The concept of T-shirt sizes simplifies the pricing and sizing in HANA.

242: What are the different T-shirt sizes available in SAP HANA?

Answer:

XS, S, S+, M, M+, L and XL are the different T-shirt sizes available in SAP HANA.

243: How does size S differ from S+ in SAP HANA?

Answer:

The T-shirt sizes S+ and M+ denote upgradable versions of the S and M sizes.

The capacity of S+ is equivalent to that of S, but the hardware is upgradable to an M size (similarly with M+, the hardware is upgradable to an L size).

244: How is disk sizing done in SAP HANA?
Answer:
The disk storage in SAP HANA has two parts:
a) **Disk persistence**
   The persistence layer writes any changes or updates in the HANA database to the disk storage in regular intervals. The capacity for this is based on the total amount of RAM (C) as: Disk persistence = 4 * C
b) **Disk log**
   Disk log contains the database logs written to non-volatile storage devices. The capacity for this is based on the total amount of RAM (C) as: Disk log = 1 * C

245: What are the available SAP HANA software licensing editions?
Answer:
The different software licensing editions available in SAP HANA are:
a) SAP HANA platform edition
b) SAP HANA enterprise edition
c) SAP HANA extended enterprise edition
d) SAP HANA solution

246: Which is lowest license edition and what options does it include?
Answer:
The platform edition is the basic edition which includes the SAP HANA database, SAP HANA Studio, SAP HANA clients and software infrastructure components. The license has to be acquired from SAP, whereas the hardware will be provided by SAP's hardware partners.

247: What extra options does the enterprise license edition offer?
Answer:
The enterprise license edition includes all the options in the platform edition plus SAP LT replication or BODS for ETL-based replication.

248: What extra options does the extended enterprise license edition offer?
Answer:
The extended enterprise license edition includes all the options in the enterprise edition plus Sybase license needed for Log-Based Replication.

249: What is included in SAP HANA solution edition?
Answer:
The SAP HANA solution offers all the options in the extended enterprise edition plus SAP Business Objects BI tools for Reporting.

250: While migrating from SAP BWA to SAP HANA, can the customers upgrade their existing licenses to SAP HANA?
Answer:
Though BWA and HANA are separately licensed products, SAP offers some credits for the existing SAP BWA licenses to be moved to SAP HANA.

HR Questions

Review these typical interview questions and think about how you would answer them. Read the answers listed; you will find best possible answers along with strategies and suggestions.

1: Where do you find ideas?

Answer:

Ideas can come from all places, and an interviewer wants to see that your ideas are just as varied. Mention multiple places that you gain ideas from, or settings in which you find yourself brainstorming. Additionally, elaborate on how you record ideas or expand upon them later.

2: How do you achieve creativity in the workplace?

Answer:

It's important to show the interviewer that you're capable of being resourceful and innovative in the workplace, without stepping outside the lines of company values. Explain where ideas normally stem from for you (examples may include an exercise such as list-making or a mind map), and connect this to a particular task in your job that it would be helpful to be creative in.

3: How do you push others to create ideas?

Answer:

If you're in a supervisory position, this may be requiring employees to submit a particular number of ideas, or to complete regular idea-generating exercises, in order to work their creative muscles. However, you can also push others around you to create ideas simply by creating more of your own. Additionally, discuss with the interviewer the importance of questioning people as a way to inspire ideas and change.

4: Describe your creativity.

Answer:

Try to keep this answer within the professional realm, but if you have an impressive background in something creative outside of your employment history, don't be afraid to include it in your answer also. The best answers about creativity will relate problem-solving skills, goal-setting, and finding innovative ways to tackle a project or make a sale in the workplace. However, passions outside of the office are great, too (so long as they don't cut into your work time or mental space).

5: Would you rather receive more authority or more responsibility at work?
Answer:
There are pros and cons to each of these options, and your interviewer will be more interested to see that you can provide a critical answer to the question. Receiving more authority may mean greater decision-making power and may be great for those with outstanding leadership skills, while greater responsibility may be a growth opportunity for those looking to advance steadily throughout their careers.

6: What do you do when someone in a group isn't contributing their fair share?
Answer:
This is a particularly important question if you're interviewing for a position in a supervisory role – explain the ways in which you would identify the problem, and how you would go about pulling aside the individual to discuss their contributions. It's important to understand the process of creating a dialogue, so that you can communicate your expectations clearly to the individual, give them a chance to respond, and to make clear what needs to change. After this, create an action plan with the group member to ensure their contributions are on par with others in the group.

7: Tell me about a time when you made a decision that was outside of your authority.
Answer:
While an answer to this question may portray you as being decisive and confident, it could also identify you to an employer as a potential problem employee. Instead, it may be best to slightly refocus the question into an example of a time that you took on additional responsibilities, and thus had to make decisions that were outside of your normal authority (but which

had been granted to you in the specific instance). Discuss how the weight of the decision affected your decision-making process, and the outcomes of the situation.

8: Are you comfortable going to supervisors with disputes?

Answer:
If a problem arises, employers want to know that you will handle it in a timely and appropriate manner. Emphasize that you've rarely had disputes with supervisors in the past, but if a situation were to arise, you feel perfectly comfortable in discussing it with the person in question in order to find a resolution that is satisfactory to both parties.

9: If you had been in charge at your last job, what would you have done differently?

Answer:
No matter how many ideas you have about how things could run better, or opinions on the management at your previous job, remain positive when answering this question. It's okay to show thoughtful reflection on how something could be handled in order to increase efficiency or improve sales, but be sure to keep all of your suggestions focused on making things better, rather than talking about ways to eliminate waste or negativity.

10: Do you believe employers should praise or reward employees for a job well done?

Answer:
Recognition is always great after completing a difficult job, but there are many employers who may ask this question as a way to infer as to whether or not you'll be a high-maintenance worker. While you may appreciate rewards or praise, it's important to convey to the interviewer that you don't require accolades to be confident that you've done your job well. If you are interviewing for a supervisory position where you would be the one praising other employees, highlight the importance of praise in boosting team morale.

11: What do you believe is the most important quality a leader can have?

Answer:

There are many important skills for a leader to have in any business, and the most important component of this question is that you explain why the quality you choose to highlight is important. Try to choose a quality such as communication skills, or an ability to inspire people, and relate it to a specific instance in which you displayed the quality among a team of people.

12: Tell me about a time when an unforeseen problem arose. How did you handle it?

Answer:

It's important that you are resourceful, and level-headed under pressure. An interviewer wants to see that you handle problems systematically, and that you can deal with change in an orderly process. Outline the situation clearly, including all solutions and results of the process you implemented.

13: Can you give me an example of a time when you were able to improve *X objective* at your previous job?

Answer:

It's important here to focus on an improvement you made that created tangible results for your company. Increasing efficiency is certainly a very important element in business, but employers are also looking for concrete results such as increased sales or cut expenses. Explain your process thoroughly, offering specific numbers and evidence wherever possible, particularly in outlining the results.

14: Tell me about a time when a supervisor did not provide specific enough direction on a project.

Answer:

While many employers want their employees to follow very specific guidelines without much decision-making power, it's important also to be able to pick up a project with vague direction and to perform self-sufficiently. Give examples of necessary questions that you asked, and specify how you determined whether a question was something you needed to ask of a supervisor or whether it was something you could determine on your own.

15: Tell me about a time when you were in charge of leading a project.

Answer:

Lead the interviewer through the process of the project, just as you would have with any of your team members. Explain the goal of the project, the necessary steps, and how you delegated tasks to your team. Include the results, and what you learned as a result of the leadership opportunity.

16: Tell me about a suggestion you made to a former employer that was later implemented.

Answer:

Employers want to see that you're interested in improving your company and doing your part – offer a specific example of something you did to create a positive change in your previous job. Explain how you thought of the idea, how your supervisors received it, and what other employees thought was the idea was put into place.

17: Tell me about a time when you thought of a way something in the workplace could be done more efficiently.

Answer:

Focus on the positive aspects of your idea. It's important not to portray your old company or boss negatively, so don't elaborate on how inefficient a particular system was. Rather, explain a situation in which you saw an opportunity to increase productivity or to streamline a process, and explain in a general step-by-step how you implemented a better system.

18: Is there a difference between leading and managing people –

which is your greater strength?

Answer:

There is a difference – leaders are often great idea people, passionate, charismatic, and with the ability to organize and inspire others, while managers are those who ensure a system runs, facilitate its operations, make authoritative decisions, and who take great responsibility for all aspects from overall success to the finest decisions. Consider which of these is most applicable to the position, and explain how you fit into this role, offering concrete examples of your past experience.

19: Do you function better in a leadership role, or as a worker on a team?

Answer:

It is important to consider what qualities the interviewer is looking for in your position, and to express how you embody this role. If you're a leader, highlight your great ideas, drive and passion, and ability to incite others around you to action. If you work great in teams, focus on your dedication to the task at hand, your cooperation and communication skills, and your ability to keep things running smoothly.

20: Tell me about a time when you discovered something in the workplace that was disrupting your (or others) productivity – what did you do about it?

Answer:

Try to not focus on negative aspects of your previous job too much, but instead choose an instance in which you found a positive, and quick, solution to increase productivity. Focus on the way you noticed the opportunity, how you presented a solution to your supervisor, and then how the change was implemented (most importantly, talk about how you led the change initiative). This is a great opportunity for you to display your problem-solving skills, as well as your resourceful nature and leadership skills.

21: How do you perform in a job with clearly-defined objectives and goals?

Answer:

It is important to consider the position when answering this question – clearly, it is best if you can excel in a job with clearly-defined objectives and goals (particularly if you're in an entry level or sales position). However, if you're applying for a position with a leadership role or creative aspect to it, be sure to focus on the ways that you additionally enjoy the challenges of developing and implementing your own ideas.

22: How do you perform in a job where you have great decision-making power?

Answer:

The interviewer wants to know that, if hired, you won't be the type of employee who needs constant supervision or who asks for advice, authority, or feedback every step of the way. Explain that you work well in a decisive, productive environment, and that you look forward to taking initiative in your position.

23: If you saw another employee doing something dishonest or unethical, what would you do?

Answer:

In the case of witnessing another employee doing something dishonest, it is always best to act in accordance with company policies for such a situation – and if you don't know what this company's specific policies are, feel free to simply state that you would handle it according to the policy and by reporting it to the appropriate persons in charge. If you are aware of the company's policies (such as if you are seeking a promotion within your own company), it is best to specifically outline your actions according to the policy.

24: Tell me about a time when you learned something on your own that later helped in your professional life.

Answer:

This question is important because it allows the interviewer to gain insight into your dedication to learning and advancement. Choose an example solely from your personal life, and provide a brief anecdote ending in the lesson you learned. Then, explain in a clear and thorough manner how this lesson has translated into a usable skill or practice in your position.

25: Tell me about a time when you developed a project idea at work.

Answer:

Choose a project idea that you developed that was typical of projects you might complete in the new position. Outline where your idea came from, the type of research you did to ensure its success and relevancy, steps that were included in the project, and the end results. Offer specific before and after statistics, to show its success.

26: Tell me about a time when you took a risk on a project.

Answer:

Whether the risk involved something as complex as taking on a major project with limited resources or time, or simply volunteering for a task that was outside your field of experience, show that you are willing to stretch out of your comfort zone and to try new things. Offer specific examples of why something you did was risky, and explain what you learned in the process – or how this prepared you for a job objective you later faced in your career.

27: What would you tell someone who was looking to get into this field?

Answer:

This question allows you to be the expert – and will show the interviewer that you have the knowledge and experience to go along with any training and education on your resume. Offer your knowledge as advice of unexpected things that someone entering the field may encounter, and be sure to end with positive advice such as the passion or dedication to the work that is required to truly succeed.

28: Tell me about a time when you didn't meet a deadline.
Answer:
Ideally, this hasn't happened – but if it has, make sure you use a minor example to illustrate the situation, emphasize how long ago it happened, and be sure that you did as much as you could to ensure that the deadline was met. Additionally, be sure to include what you learned about managing time better or prioritizing tasks in order to meet all future deadlines.

29: How do you eliminate distractions while working?
Answer:
With the increase of technology and the ease of communication, new distractions arise every day. Your interviewer will want to see that you are still able to focus on work, and that your productivity has not been affected, by an example showing a routine you employ in order to stay on task.

30: Tell me about a time when you worked in a position with a weekly or monthly quota to meet. How often were you successful?
Answer:
Your numbers will speak for themselves, and you must answer this question honestly. If you were regularly met your quotas, be sure to highlight this in a confident manner and don't be shy in pointing out your strengths in this area. If your statistics are less than stellar, try to point out trends in which they increased toward the end of your employment, and show reflection as to ways you can improve in the future.

31: Tell me about a time when you met a tough deadline, and how you were able to complete it.
Answer:
Explain how you were able to prioritize tasks, or to delegate

portions of an assignments to other team members, in order to deal with a tough deadline. It may be beneficial to specify why the deadline was tough – make sure it's clear that it was not a result of procrastination on your part. Finally, explain how you were able to successfully meet the deadline, and what it took to get there in the end.

32: How do you stay organized when you have multiple projects on your plate?

Answer:
The interviewer will be looking to see that you can manage your time and work well – and being able to handle multiple projects at once, and still giving each the attention it deserves, is a great mark of a worker's competence and efficiency. Go through a typical process of goal-setting and prioritizing, and explain the steps of these to the interviewer, so he or she can see how well you manage time.

33: How much time during your work day do you spend on "auto-pilot?"

Answer:
While you may wonder if the employer is looking to see how efficient you are with this question (for example, so good at your job that you don't have to think about it), but in almost every case, the employer wants to see that you're constantly thinking, analyzing, and processing what's going on in the workplace. Even if things are running smoothly, there's usually an opportunity somewhere to make things more efficient or to increase sales or productivity. Stress your dedication to ongoing development, and convey that being on "auto-pilot" is not conducive to that type of success.

34: How do you handle deadlines?

Answer:
The most important part of handling tough deadlines is to prioritize tasks and set goals for completion, as well as to delegate

or eliminate unnecessary work. Lead the interviewer through a general scenario, and display your competency through your ability to organize and set priorities, and most importantly, remain calm.

35: Tell me about your personal problem-solving process.
Answer:
Your personal problem-solving process should include outlining the problem, coming up with possible ways to fix the problem, and setting a clear action plan that leads to resolution. Keep your answer brief and organized, and explain the steps in a concise, calm manner that shows you are level-headed even under stress.

36: What sort of things at work can make you stressed?
Answer:
As it's best to stay away from negatives, keep this answer brief and simple. While answering that nothing at work makes you stressed will not be very believable to the interviewer, keep your answer to one generic principle such as when members of a team don't keep their commitments, and then focus on a solution you generally employ to tackle that stress, such as having weekly status meetings or intermittent deadlines along the course of a project.

37: What do you look like when you are stressed about something? How do you solve it?
Answer:
This is a trick question – your interviewer wants to hear that you don't look any different when you're stressed, and that you don't allow negative emotions to interfere with your productivity. As far as how you solve your stress, it's best if you have a simple solution mastered, such as simply taking deep breaths and counting to 10 to bring yourself back to the task at hand.

38: Can you multi-task?
Answer:

Some people can, and some people can't. The most important part of multi-tasking is to keep a clear head at all times about what needs to be done, and what priority each task falls under. Explain how you evaluate tasks to determine priority, and how you manage your time in order to ensure that all are completed efficiently.

39: How many hours per week do you work?

Answer:

Many people get tricked by this question, thinking that answering more hours is better – however, this may cause an employer to wonder why you have to work so many hours in order to get the work done that other people can do in a shorter amount of time. Give a fair estimate of hours that it should take you to complete a job, and explain that you are also willing to work extra whenever needed.

40: How many times per day do you check your email?

Answer:

While an employer wants to see that you are plugged into modern technology, it is also important that the number of times you check your email per day is relatively low – perhaps two to three times per day (dependent on the specific field you're in). Checking email is often a great distraction in the workplace, and while it is important to remain connected, much correspondence can simply be handled together in the morning and afternoon.

41: Describe a time when you communicated a difficult or complicated idea to a coworker.

Answer:

Start by explaining the idea briefly to the interviewer, and then give an overview of why it was necessary to break it down further to the coworker. Finally, explain the idea in succinct steps, so the interviewer can see your communication abilities and skill in simplification.

42: What situations do you find it difficult to communicate in?

Answer:
Even great communicators will often find particular situations that are more difficult to communicate effectively in, so don't be afraid to answer this question honestly. Be sure to explain why the particular situation you name is difficult for you, and try to choose an uncommon answer such as language barrier or in time of hardship, rather than a situation such as speaking to someone of higher authority.

43: What are the key components of good communication?

Answer:
Some of the components of good communication include an environment that is free from distractions, feedback from the listener, and revision or clarification from the speaker when necessary. Refer to basic communication models where necessary, and offer to go through a role-play sample with the interviewer in order to show your skills.

44: Tell me about a time when you solved a problem through communication?

Answer:
Solving problems through communication is key in the business world, so choose a specific situation from your previous job in which you navigated a messy situation by communicating effectively through the conflict. Explain the basis of the situation, as well as the communication steps you took, and end with a discussion of why communicating through the problem was so important to its resolution.

45: Tell me about a time when you had a dispute with another employee. How did you resolve the situation?

Answer:
Make sure to use a specific instance, and explain step-by-step the scenario, what you did to handle it, and how it was finally resolved. The middle step, how you handled the dispute, is clearly

the most definitive – describe the types of communication you used, and how you used compromise to reach a decision. Conflict resolution is an important skill for any employee to have, and is one that interviewers will search for to determine both how likely you are to be involved in disputes, and how likely they are to be forced to become involved in the dispute if one arises.

46: Do you build relationships quickly with people, or take more time to get to know them?
Answer:
Either of these options can display good qualities, so determine which style is more applicable to you. Emphasize the steps you take in relationship-building over the particular style, and summarize briefly why this works best for you.

47: Describe a time when you had to work through office politics to solve a problem.
Answer:
Try to focus on the positives in this question, so that you can use the situation to your advantage. Don't portray your previous employer negatively, and instead use a minimal instance (such as paperwork or a single individual), to highlight how you worked through a specific instance resourcefully. Give examples of communication skills or problem-solving you used in order to achieve a resolution.

48: Tell me about a time when you persuaded others to take on a difficult task?
Answer:
This question is an opportunity to highlight both your leadership and communication skills. While the specific situation itself is important to offer as background, focus on how you were able to persuade the others, and what tactics worked the best.

49: Tell me about a time when you successfully persuaded a group to accept your proposal.

Answer:
This question is designed to determine your resourcefulness and your communication skills. Explain the ways in which you took into account different perspectives within the group, and created a presentation that would be appealing and convincing to all members. Additionally, you can pump up the proposal itself by offering details about it that show how well-executed it was.

50: Tell me about a time when you had a problem with another person, that, in hindsight, you wished you had handled differently.
Answer:
The key to this question is to show your capabilities of reflection and your learning process. Explain the situation, how you handled it at the time, what the outcome of the situation was, and finally, how you would handle it now. Most importantly, tell the interviewer why you would handle it differently now – did your previous solution create stress on the relationship with the other person, or do you wish that you had stood up more for what you wanted? While you shouldn't elaborate on how poorly you handled the situation before, the most important thing is to show that you've grown and reached a deeper level of understanding as a result of the conflict.

51: Tell me about a time when you negotiated a conflict between other employees.
Answer:
An especially important question for those interviewing for a supervisory role – begin with a specific situation, and explain how you communicated effectively to each individual. For example, did you introduce a compromise? Did you make an executive decision? Or, did you perform as a mediator and encourage the employees to reach a conclusion on their own?

INDEX

SAP HANA Interview Questions

General Overview

1: What led to the invention of SAP HANA technology?
2: Which technologies did SAP HANA evolve from?
3: Is SAP HANA a software or hardware?
4: What are the main components in SAP HANA?
5: What is SAP HANA?
6: What are the capabilities and benefits that HANA offers?
7: What are the basic technology concepts in SAP HANA?
8: What is the benefit of In-Memory in SAP HANA?
9: Why is SAP HANA fast?
10: What is columnar storage and how does it support faster access of data?
11: Are column-based tables always better than row-based tables?
12: What is the difference between row store and column store?
13: Can you have row store tables in SAP HANA?
14: How do you decide if the table should be row or column store in your project?
15: How does insert or update work faster in HANA environment?
16: What degree of data compression is expected in SAP HANA?
17: What is Delta Merge and how does it support faster read operations?
18: What are the different ways of performing delta merge operation?
19: When you run a query before delta merge, will you lose the data in the delta storage in the result set?
20: What is memory latency and how does it hit the performance?
21: How does SAP HANA handle the latency problem?
22: How does SAP HANA support parallel processing?
23: Which are the top use cases in SAP HANA?
24: What is the difference between SAP BWA and SAP HANA?

Architecture

25: What are the primary prerequisites for SAP BW on HANA?
26: What is the Operating System requirement for SAP HANA?
27: Can HANA Server be configured via Scale up or Scale out configurations?

28: Name the servers operational in a HANA database.

29: What is the role of each server in the HANA database?

30: What are the different services present in the HANA appliance?

31: What is the functionality of SUM and LM structures?

32: Which component coordinates and tracks the database transactions?

33: How is an application query processed by the Index Server in SAP HANA?

34: What is the role of MDX engine in the HANA server?

35: Which are the two relational engines in In-Memory Computing Engine?

36: What are the key architecture points to be considered to ensure business continuity?

37: How does HANA hardware support High Data Availability?

38: How is HANA hardware structured towards Disaster Tolerance?

39: What is Scale-Out approach?

40: How is the Scale-Out architecture configured in HANA environment?

41: Which services will be active on each of the nodes in a scale-out landscape?

42: How is Master Name server failure handled in the distributed landscape?

43: How is Master Index server failure handled in the distributed landscape?

44: What is the significance of XS Engine (Extended Application Service)?

Data Provisioning

45: What are the different replication scenarios available in SAP HANA?

46: What are the different types of Data Provisioning supported by SAP HANA?

47: Which tool provides trigger based replication services?

48: What are the key benefits of SLT Replication or Trigger-Based Approach?

49: When should a customer go for SLT over other replication methods?

50: What are the technologies used by SLT Replication Server?

51: Which connection method is used between Source System and the SAP LT Replication Server?

52: Which connection method is used between SAP LT Replication Server and SAP HANA system?

53: Should SAP LT Replication Server be a separate system always?

54: What is the prerequisite while installing SAP LT Replication Server?

55: What is the recommended method of installing SAP LT Replication

Server?

56: Which technology supports real-time replication of SAP Cluster tables into HANA database?

57: A single source system can be connected to several target schemas in SLT, what is the maximum limit?

58: What is the purpose of DB trigger in SLT?

59: What is the purpose of Controller Module in SLT?

60: Which tool supports ETL based replication into HANA?

61: What are the advantages of using BODS to load data into SAP HANA?

62: What are the limitations while using BODS for data replication?

63: Which SAP ECC table stores the extractors' information used in Data Services?

64: Which file types are supported in flat file upload to SAP HANA database?

65: What are the steps to follow to upload a flat file into HANA?

66: Which are the two options available for target table during flat file upload?

67: Which is the most relevant control tables involved in SLT replication?

68: What are the parameters required to configure SLT for replicating SAP data into HANA database?

69: What are the scheduling options available while configuring SLT?

70: In the data replication options, what is the difference between Stop and Suspend Replication?

71: What are the types of Transformation Rules available in SLT replication?

72: Which replication method uses ODP (Operational Data Provider) for data replication?

73: What are the benefits of ODP in Data Services?

74: Which transaction is used for releasing extractors specified by the customers?

75: What are the different methods in Data Services for extracting data from SAP applications?

76: Which dataflow in BODS is used to extract large volumes of data from SAP ECC?

Modeling

77: What are the credentials you need to add a system to SAP HANA Studio?

78: Which all folders do you see after logging into HANA Studio?

79: Do the information models store data in SAP HANA?

80: How does HANA minimize data duplication?

81: What are perspectives in HANA Studio and how are they relevant?

82: Which perspective should you select to create data models in HANA?

83: How will you change the connection to another HANA system within Studio?

84: What are the different types of views that you deal with in SAP HANA modeling?

85: What is an Attribute View? Brief on.

86: What is an Analytic View? Brief on.

87: What is a Calculation View? Brief on.

88: What are the types of Attribute Views?

89: What are the types of Calculation Views?

90: While creating an Attribute View, you will have options as 'Standard and 'Derived', what is the difference between the two?

91: What are the properties of a derived attribute view?

92: The Script Based Calculation View can be written in two ways, what are they?

93: What is mandatory in an Attribute View without which you cannot activate it?

94: What is mandatory in an Analytic View without which you cannot activate it?

95: What are the conditions to follow while selecting measures in an Analytic View?

96: SAP HANA appliance comes with different types of engines, what are they?

97: Where do the information models get created in HANA?

98: How will you query data from the information models in HANA?

99: Which schema holds the metadata information in SAP HANA?

100: What are the different ways to preview data in an information view?

101: What options do you get while doing Data Preview?

102: List the different types of Joins available in SAP HANA.

103: What should you be aware of while using Inner Joins?

104: Which are the fastest and slowest joins in SAP HANA context?

105: What is a Referential Join? Explain.

106: Why should Referential Joins be used with caution?

107: Right outer join is rarely used, give a business case where Right Outer Join would be used.

108: What are the join properties to be defined while connecting two tables?

109: Define Cardinality and its different types.

110: Explain about Text Join in SAP HANA.

111: Give a SAP example where you can use Text Join.

112: What are the best practices to be followed while connecting tables in HANA?

113: Mention few cases where activating the analytic model would result in error.

114: Is self joins possible in SAP HANA?

115: How will you resolve the "self join detected on table" error in an analytic view?

116: Why is it advised to ensure decreasing cardinality going from the center of the star schema to the outside?

117: Briefly mention the steps involved in creating a simple Analytic View.

118: Which folder cannot be accessed from the Administrator Console?

119: What are the different types of objects under a package?

120: Which calendars can be created using Time Attribute views?

121: What are the different components in a Graphical Calculation view?

122: How is Currency Conversion supported in HANA?

123: Which is the preferred way of doing Currency Conversion?

124: What is the prerequisite to enable the currency conversion functionality?

125: Which transaction code is used to get the table relationships in SAP ERP?

126: What are the cons of using Inner Join in information models?

127: In which scenarios can Inner Join give better performance?

128: If there are filters and joins included in a view, how does the query get executed on the same?

129: What is Full Outer Join and how is it supported in SAP HANA?

130: Which join property is defined only for Text Joins while connecting tables?

131: What are Temporal Joins?

132: How do you create a Temporal Join in an information model?

133: What are the limitations of Temporal Join in HANA?

134: Is Temporal Join supported by all versions of SAP HANA?

135: In Script Based Calculation Views what is recommended to be used, the built in functions or SQL?

136: Out of Union and Join, which is preferred in a Calculation View?

137: In which view should joins be implemented to get better performance?

138: Which is the best place to create calculated attributes?

139: Where can the UNION function be realized in HANA?

140: How will you combine multiple Analytic Views without impacting the performance of your query?

141: How is Union with Constant values different from Standard Union?

142: What is the main difference between UNION in graphical view and CE_UNION_ALL function in Script Based Calculation View?

143: What are the advantages of Graphical Calculation View over Script Based Calculation View?

144: How do you create copies of an existing model?

145: What is the Refactor option available for a view?

146: What are the different types of measures in HANA?

147: What are Restricted Columns?

148: How will you to create a Restricted Column in an Attribute View?

149: How do you create stand alone Text Tables in an Attribute View?

150: Are Hierarchies supported in SAP HANA?

151: How are the two Hierarchy types different?

152: What are the key points to remember while creating a Hierarchy in HANA?

153: Where do you define Hierarchies in HANA Studio?

154: How can you enforce calculations at each line item before aggregation of Measures?

155: What content does the Auto Documentation include and in which format?

156: In which scenario will you build a calculation view with SQL script rather than the graphical one?

157: Which component breaks the SQL query into executable parts?

158: What is the functionality of SQL Optimizer?

159: Describe few best practices while creating Script Based Calculation Views.

160: How does mixing of SQL and CE operators impact the performance?

161: What are the different ways to filter data at the lower layers while modeling?

162: How are Filters different from WHERE clause?

163: Is it possible to create dynamic filters in an information model?

164: What is the difference between Variables and Input Parameters?

165: Describe the different Table Types available in HANA.

166: What is the significance of History Column table?

167: How do you query from a History Table to get time travelled data?

168: Procedures are created using executable rights, what are the two

types of rights?
169: How is the Definer mode different from Invoker mode in procedures?
170: How can you preview the data results of a Procedure?
171: What are the different CE functions used to read data from an information model?
172: What are the failure modes available in Currency Conversion?
173: What are the prerequisites to enable user prompt for target currency in Currency Conversion?
174: How is Currency Conversion done in Calculation Views?
175: What is Fuzzy Search and how is it supported in HANA?
176: Which data types does Fuzzy Search support?
177: How does HANA speed up the fuzzy search functionality?
178: What is the relevance of Fuzzy Score?
179: How is fuzzy search realized using SQL query?
180: How will you check the model dependencies while changing or deleting information objects?
181: Is versioning of models possible in HANA?
182: What is a Delivery Unit and how is it relevant?
183: How many types of Import/Export are possible in HANA?
184: How is Client-Side Import different from Server-Side Import of information models?
185: What is the significance of Life Cycle Management in SAP HANA?
186: What are the steps involved to implement SAP HANA appliance?
187: How is the SAP delivered content Information model accessed?
188: What is the relevance of Schema Mapping?

Security and Authorization
189: What are the different types of privileges in SAP HANA?
190: What is the privilege required to access data from the activated views?
191: Which Authentication Methods are supported by SAP HANA?
192: What are the steps involved in managing users and roles in Security?
193: Which single-sign-on (SSO) authentication method is supported by SAP HANA?

Reporting
195: Which are the reporting tools supported by HANA?
196: Which database clients are available to connect to SAP HANA?
197: Which web-based interfaces support HANA connectivity?

198: Which connectivity methods support reporting off HANA?

199: Which drivers connect to HANA database via SQL?

200: Which driver uses MDX Connectivity to HANA?

201: How do BICS drivers connect to HANA?

202: Which reporting tools use ODBC or JDBC driver connectivity?

203: Which reporting tools use ODBO driver connectivity?

204: Which reporting tools use SQL DBC driver or BICS?

205: Which tool is used to create BI Universes for Reporting?

206: Which Connectivity supports Hierarchies in SAP HANA models?

207: In which scenario will users go for reporting in MS Excel?

208: What is the significance of Crystal Reports?

209: What is the significance of Dashboards?

210: Which reporting tool allows ad hoc reporting and interacts with information?

211: What are the advantages of Webi reporting?

212: Which reporting tool allows complex reporting on historical data to determine trends and make forecasts?

213: What are the advantages of reporting through BI Explorer?

214: What are the mandatory steps to be followed to use Explorer with SAP HANA for reporting?

215: Which reporting tools connect through BI Universe to SAP HANA?

216: What are the steps involved in creating a Universe through IDT?

217: What are the objects accessible while creating an IDT Data Foundation?

218: What is the purpose of SAP HANA Information Composer?

Backup and Recovery

219: Which database concept will be violated by in-memory in SAP HANA?

220: How does SAP HANA ensure data reliability using in-memory?

221: What is the significance of the persistence layer in SAP HANA?

222: Which are the components in the persistence layer?

223: Which are the components in the disk storage layer?

224: What are redo and undo logs?

225: How does the persistence layer work in SAP HANA?

226: What are the recovery steps to follow after reboot or power failure which deletes in-memory data?

227: What are the prerequisites to restore the SAP HANA system after restart?

228: What are the different kinds of backup in SAP HANA?

229: What is the system prerequisite for backup and recovery?

230: In which scenario do we need backup and recovery?

231: What is the procedure followed for database copy using backups?

232: What are the different data sources involved in the recovery process?

233: What are the steps to follow during recovery to last committed state?

234: What are the different recovery scenarios available in HANA?

235: What is point-in-time recovery?

236: How is point-in-time recovery done in HANA, recovery to state of database at time t1?

237: If the log area is damaged, to which state can the system be recovered?

238: During the database recovery process, will the SAP HANA system be available?

Pricing and Licensing

239: How is the SAP HANA appliance priced?

240: Give a brief on SAP HANA sizing.

241: Why is the concept of T-shirt sizes significant in SAP HANA?

242: What are the different T-shirt sizes available in SAP HANA?

243: How does size S differ from S+ in SAP HANA?

244: How is disk sizing done in SAP HANA?

245: What are the available SAP HANA software licensing editions?

246: Which is lowest license edition and what options does it include?

247: What extra options does the enterprise license edition offer?

248: What extra options does the extended enterprise license edition offer?

249: What is included in SAP HANA solution edition?

250: While migrating from SAP BWA to SAP HANA, can the customers upgrade their existing licenses to SAP HANA?

HR Questions

1: Where do you find ideas?

2: How do you achieve creativity in the workplace?

3: How do you push others to create ideas?

4: Describe your creativity.

5: Would you rather receive more authority or more responsibility at work?

6: What do you do when someone in a group isn't contributing their fair share?

7: Tell me about a time when you made a decision that was outside of your authority.

8: Are you comfortable going to supervisors with disputes?

9: If you had been in charge at your last job, what would you have done differently?

10: Do you believe employers should praise or reward employees for a job well done?

11: What do you believe is the most important quality a leader can have?

12: Tell me about a time when an unforeseen problem arose. How did you handle it?

13: Can you give me an example of a time when you were able to improve X objective at your previous job?

14: Tell me about a time when a supervisor did not provide specific enough direction on a project.

15: Tell me about a time when you were in charge of leading a project.

16: Tell me about a suggestion you made to a former employer that was later implemented.

17: Tell me about a time when you thought of a way something in the workplace could be done more efficiently.

18: Is there a difference between leading and managing people – which is your greater strength?

19: Do you function better in a leadership role, or as a worker on a team?

20: Tell me about a time when you discovered something in the workplace that was disrupting your (or others) productivity – what did you do about it?

21: How do you perform in a job with clearly-defined objectives and goals?

22: How do you perform in a job where you have great decision-making power?

23: If you saw another employee doing something dishonest or unethical, what would you do?

24: Tell me about a time when you learned something on your own that later helped in your professional life.

25: Tell me about a time when you developed a project idea at work.

26: Tell me about a time when you took a risk on a project.

27: What would you tell someone who was looking to get into this field?

28: Tell me about a time when you didn't meet a deadline.

29: How do you eliminate distractions while working?

30: Tell me about a time when you worked in a position with a weekly or monthly quota to meet. How often were you successful?

31: Tell me about a time when you met a tough deadline, and how you were able to complete it.

32: How do you stay organized when you have multiple projects on your plate?

33: How much time during your work day do you spend on "auto-pilot?"

34: How do you handle deadlines?

35: Tell me about your personal problem-solving process.

36: What sort of things at work can make you stressed?

37: What do you look like when you are stressed about something? How do you solve it?

38: Can you multi-task?

39: How many hours per week do you work?

40: How many times per day do you check your email?

41: Describe a time when you communicated a difficult or complicated idea to a coworker.

42: What situations do you find it difficult to communicate in?

43: What are the key components of good communication?

44: Tell me about a time when you solved a problem through communication?

45: Tell me about a time when you had a dispute with another employee. How did you resolve the situation?

46: Do you build relationships quickly with people, or take more time to get to know them?

47: Describe a time when you had to work through office politics to solve a problem.

48: Tell me about a time when you persuaded others to take on a difficult task?

49: Tell me about a time when you successfully persuaded a group to accept your proposal.

50: Tell me about a time when you had a problem with another person, that, in hindsight, you wished you had handled differently.

51: Tell me about a time when you negotiated a conflict between other employees.

Some of the following titles might also be handy:

1. .NET Interview Questions You'll Most Likely Be Asked
2. 200 Interview Questions You'll Most Likely Be Asked
3. Access VBA Programming Interview Questions You'll Most Likely Be Asked
4. Adobe ColdFusion Interview Questions You'll Most Likely Be Asked
5. Advanced Excel Interview Questions You'll Most Likely Be Asked
6. Advanced Java Interview Questions You'll Most Likely Be Asked
7. Advanced SAS Interview Questions You'll Most Likely Be Asked
8. AJAX Interview Questions You'll Most Likely Be Asked
9. Algorithms Interview Questions You'll Most Likely Be Asked
10. Android Development Interview Questions You'll Most Likely Be Asked
11. Ant & Maven Interview Questions You'll Most Likely Be Asked
12. Apache Web Server Interview Questions You'll Most Likely Be Asked
13. Artificial Intelligence Interview Questions You'll Most Likely Be Asked
14. ASP.NET Interview Questions You'll Most Likely Be Asked
15. Automated Software Testing Interview Questions You'll Most Likely Be Asked
16. Base SAS Interview Questions You'll Most Likely Be Asked
17. BEA WebLogic Server Interview Questions You'll Most Likely Be Asked
18. C & C++ Interview Questions You'll Most Likely Be Asked
19. C# Interview Questions You'll Most Likely Be Asked
20. C++ Internals Interview Questions You'll Most Likely Be Asked
21. CCNA Interview Questions You'll Most Likely Be Asked
22. Cloud Computing Interview Questions You'll Most Likely Be Asked
23. Computer Architecture Interview Questions You'll Most Likely Be Asked
24. Computer Networks Interview Questions You'll Most Likely Be Asked
25. Core Java Interview Questions You'll Most Likely Be Asked
26. Data Structures & Algorithms Interview Questions You'll Most Likely Be Asked
27. Data WareHousing Interview Questions You'll Most Likely Be Asked
28. EJB 3.0 Interview Questions You'll Most Likely Be Asked
29. Entity Framework Interview Questions You'll Most Likely Be Asked
30. Fedora & RHEL Interview Questions You'll Most Likely Be Asked
31. GNU Development Interview Questions You'll Most Likely Be Asked
32. Hibernate, Spring & Struts Interview Questions You'll Most Likely Be Asked
33. HTML, XHTML and CSS Interview Questions You'll Most Likely Be Asked
34. HTML5 Interview Questions You'll Most Likely Be Asked
35. IBM WebSphere Application Server Interview Questions You'll Most Likely Be Asked
36. iOS SDK Interview Questions You'll Most Likely Be Asked
37. Java / J2EE Design Patterns Interview Questions You'll Most Likely Be Asked
38. Java / J2EE Interview Questions You'll Most Likely Be Asked
39. Java Messaging Service Interview Questions You'll Most Likely Be Asked
40. JavaScript Interview Questions You'll Most Likely Be Asked
41. JavaServer Faces Interview Questions You'll Most Likely Be Asked
42. JDBC Interview Questions You'll Most Likely Be Asked
43. jQuery Interview Questions You'll Most Likely Be Asked
44. JSP-Servlet Interview Questions You'll Most Likely Be Asked
45. JUnit Interview Questions You'll Most Likely Be Asked
46. Linux Commands Interview Questions You'll Most Likely Be Asked
47. Linux Interview Questions You'll Most Likely Be Asked
48. Linux System Administrator Interview Questions You'll Most Likely Be Asked
49. Mac OS X Lion Interview Questions You'll Most Likely Be Asked
50. Mac OS X Snow Leopard Interview Questions You'll Most Likely Be Asked
51. Microsoft Access Interview Questions You'll Most Likely Be Asked

52. Microsoft Excel Interview Questions You'll Most Likely Be Asked
53. Microsoft Powerpoint Interview Questions You'll Most Likely Be Asked
54. Microsoft Word Interview Questions You'll Most Likely Be Asked
55. MySQL Interview Questions You'll Most Likely Be Asked
56. NetSuite Interview Questions You'll Most Likely Be Asked
57. Networking Interview Questions You'll Most Likely Be Asked
58. OOPS Interview Questions You'll Most Likely Be Asked
59. Operating Systems Interview Questions You'll Most Likely Be Asked
60. Oracle DBA Interview Questions You'll Most Likely Be Asked
61. Oracle E-Business Suite Interview Questions You'll Most Likely Be Asked
62. Oracle PL/SQL Interview Questions You'll Most Likely Be Asked
63. Perl Interview Questions You'll Most Likely Be Asked
64. PHP Interview Questions You'll Most Likely Be Asked
65. PMP Interview Questions You'll Most Likely Be Asked
66. Python Interview Questions You'll Most Likely Be Asked
67. RESTful JAVA Web Services Interview Questions You'll Most Likely Be Asked
68. Ruby Interview Questions You'll Most Likely Be Asked
69. Ruby on Rails Interview Questions You'll Most Likely Be Asked
70. SAP ABAP Interview Questions You'll Most Likely Be Asked
71. SAS STAT and Programming Interview Questions You'll Most Likely Be Asked
72. Selenium Testing Tools Interview Questions You'll Most Likely Be Asked
73. Silverlight Interview Questions You'll Most Likely Be Asked
74. Software Repositories Interview Questions You'll Most Likely Be Asked
75. Software Testing Interview Questions You'll Most Likely Be Asked
76. SQL Server Interview Questions You'll Most Likely Be Asked
77. Tomcat Interview Questions You'll Most Likely Be Asked
78. UML Interview Questions You'll Most Likely Be Asked
79. Unix Interview Questions You'll Most Likely Be Asked
80. UNIX Shell Programming Interview Questions You'll Most Likely Be Asked
81. VB.NET Interview Questions You'll Most Likely Be Asked
82. XLXP, XSLT, XPATH, XFORMS & XQuery Interview Questions You'll Most Likely Be Asked
83. XML Interview Questions You'll Most Likely Be Asked

For complete list visit

www.vibrantpublishers.com

4310254R00057

Made in the USA
San Bernardino, CA
14 September 2013